AF484675

Chapter One

WHY AM I HERE?

"How do I know what my purpose in life is?" This is a very common question on the mind of individuals all around the world both young and old, it is very important to find out what your life's mission and purpose is at an early age. Your purpose in life is far greater than your personal fulfillment, your peace of mind, or even your happiness. It's far greater than your family, your career, or even your wildest dreams and ambitions. To know why you were placed on this planet, you must begin with God. He has a purpose for His creation, there is a mission for you here on earth and until you discover why you are here on earth and fulfill that mission, you will never find fulfillment.

We must work the works of Him who sent Me and be busy with His business while its daylight, night is coming on, when no man can work – John 9:4(AMPC)

Life on its own is a journey; it's like a race in which all participants are running feverishly to achieve a goal which is their mission here on earth. We run with exuberance and tenacity to attain these goals that might seem to elude us as we want to find answers to life's mysteries before we have those questions in our face. It is imperative that we ascertain our purpose here on earth and find answers to life mysteries so that we don't become confused when life thorns show up on our faces.

Now the question is how we find out the answers to life mysteries or find out what our Mission and Purpose are here on earth. To get the answers, we must first know our source and who our creator is. Most times it's the trust and belief we have in a manufacturer that gives us some comfort in the product in case of malfunction. Since God is our creator, we must know Him, trust Him, belief, and have a relationship with Him to understand our Purpose or Mission here on earth.

We are His products, His workmanship, created in His image and He is always proud to showcase us to the world only if we can commit ourselves to know Him and have a relationship with Him.

For we are God's(own) handiwork (His workmanship), recreated in Christ Jesus (born anew) that we may do those good works which God predestined for us (taking path which He prepared ahead of time), that we should walk in them (living the good life which He prearranged and made ready for us to live). Ephesians 2:10. AMPC

It is the quest to find out our purpose on earth that drives the need to know our creator, for it is only through the knowledge of God that can we know and understand what His plan for our lives is. Therefore, we need to know God, have a relationship with Him, and understand His words, for in His word, will we find our purpose. It is through the knowledge of God's word that we will be able to find out why we are here on earth.

You can never be fulfilled if you don't know why you are here on earth or what your purpose is here on earth. You can find out about this by knowing your creator and you will find yourself in Him and your fulfillment.

Chapter Two

HOW TO FIND YOUR PURPOSE

Life purpose is a spiritual concept or has a religious dimension. For others, it's a more secular notion, a need to be valued as a member of a family or group.

A "purpose" can be as simple as your intention or a resolution. So, a "life purpose" is really nothing more (or less) than your intention to live in a certain way.

A life purpose is realized through "intention" —by getting to know your authentic self, exploring your gifts or natural talents and passions —choosing the best possible expression to share them with the world.

"Finding" your purpose can be misleading because it's not something we just go out and "get," rather it's something we need to look within and "unlock. If you want to know why you were placed on this planet, you must begin with God. You were born by His purpose and for His purpose. The search for the purpose of life has puzzled people for thousands of years. But the bible makes it clear in Job12:10

In His hand is the life of every living thing and the breath of all mankind. – (AMPC)

You cannot arrive at your life's purpose by only focusing on yourself. You must begin with God, your Creator. You only exist because He wills that you exist. You were made by Him and for Him — and until you understand that life will never make sense. It is only in Him that we discover our origin, our identity, our meaning, our purpose, our significance, and our destiny. Every other path leads to a dead end.

"Now the mind of the flesh (which is sense and reason without the Holy Spirit) is death (death that arises from all the miseries arising from sin, both here and hereafter). But the mind of the (Holy) Spirit is life and (soul) peace (both now and forever). - AMPC

God has not left us in the dark to wonder and guess. He has clearly revealed His purpose for our lives through the Bible. It is our daily Manual, explaining why we are here on earth, why we are alive, how life works, what to do, what to avoid, and what to expect in the future. It explains better than any self-help or philosophy book you know. To discover your purpose in life you must turn to God's Word, not the world's wisdom. You must build your life on eternal truths, not pop psychology, success, or inspirational stories. The Bible says,

"In Him, we also were made (God's) heritage (portion) and we obtained an inheritance; for we had been foreordained (chosen and appointed beforehand) in accordance with His purpose, who works out everything in agreement with the counsel and design of His (own) will. - Ephesians 1:11-12. AMPC.

We discover our identity and purpose through a relationship with Jesus Christ, His purpose for our life started from conception. He planned our lives before we existed, without our input! We may choose our career, our spouse, our hobbies, and many other parts of our life, but we don't get to choose our purpose. This explains that Christ is the force behind creation, we are not created by chance but of destiny. We serve a God of plan and purpose. In Jeremiah 1:5, God said

Before I formed you in the womb I knew (and) approved of you (as My chosen instrument), and before you were born, I separated and set you apart, consecrating you; (and) I appointed you as a prophet to the nations. – AMPC.

Apostle Paul also said that God separated him from his mother's womb in Galatians 1:15! He said, "But when it pleased God, who separated me from my mother's womb, and called me by His grace". God still separates people today from their mother's wombs. Your journey to discovering your purpose in life begins when you get to know God for yourself, as it was with Apostle Paul.

You can never become a star or hero until you begin to work in God's plan for your life not another's, you must work in God's plan for your life. Every creature here on earth, has a plan which was created by God before you were born, but you can only discover what your plan is or why you are here on earth when you create a relationship with God and search His words to find your place in it.

Everyone has been ordained to carry out a particular function. The Bible said we are members of the same body, but each member has a function to carry out. Joseph had a divine task, Abraham had a divine mandate, and Gideon had his own purpose. You have a divine assignment here on earth, a divine purpose, and discovery to this Purpose that gives you fulfillment in life.

Chapter Three

WHERE DOES A LIFE PURPOSE COME FROM?

It's the kind of inner journey that changes everything – from emptiness to satisfaction, from boredom to passion, from aimlessness to unbridled joy and beyond! In fact, you may be surprised to discover that realizing and living your life's purpose will be a comfortable and enjoyable process. Bit by bit, you'll create life circumstances that are totally suited to who you are, your likes and dislikes, natural talents, and much more.

One of the reasons people often doubt that they have a life purpose is because they've been led to believe that a life purpose is akin to those "spiritual callings" mentioned earlier. If they don't feel an inner calling, they decide that there probably isn't a specific purpose for their life – or worse, that their life has no meaning at all.

If you ask enough people, you'll probably find that there are two basic schools of thought regarding life purpose:

- Those who believe that a life purpose is something we are born with, that it is planted into our souls before we are born, and we MUST achieve it. It's our destiny so to speak, and we have no choice in the matter.
- Those who believe that fate and destiny don't exist, and we have the power (or "free will") to choose our life purpose and do anything we want with our lives.

Which group do you belong to? There are no right or wrong answers to this question; only what you feel in your heart is the right answer for you.

Personally, I believe that each of us has a pre-destined life purpose here on earth, remember He knew us before we were born so He had planned for us, He had created a purpose for us here on earth – BUT it is something that we must consciously work towards realizing by getting to know Him, having a relationship with Him and Him showing Himself and this life purpose to us. Life's purpose, in my opinion, is realized by getting to know your authentic self through your knowledge of His words, exploring them, and choosing the best possible medium to share them with the world.

I want you to understand something here, God has a plan for you, God has a purpose for you here on earth and the highest prize for that purpose for which you were created is a crown, a crown of fulfillment. Therefore, you owe yourself the responsibility of ascertaining the genuineness of your purpose and launching out in pursuit of it.

One of the major characteristics of a genuine life purpose is that it has its source in God, it's God's revealed plan and if you study it properly, it is traceable to God. Any purpose that does not have its source in God leads to destruction, it might flourish for a while but certainly, destruction is inevitable.

Absalom, the son of David had a desire which he took as his life purpose. He wanted to become a king so much that he couldn't wait for his father to die, His comportment and appearance made him gain approval from the people. Being pushed on by his own self-made purpose and desire, he declared himself king. This was not God's purpose for him, for a while everything around him looked sweet and rosy but suddenly destruction came in 2 Samuel.

Every purpose that is from God leads to glorification but anyone that is not from Him leads to destruction. Take a cue from King David. He had a divine calling, a divine purpose, he was anointed king in place of Saul, but if Saul was alive, David never sought to take the throne away, he only ran away when it was clear that his life was in danger. When your plan and purpose are in line with God's agenda for you, He will create a peaceful way for you to achieve it in His own time. Every God's given purpose is characterized by peace, any plan or purpose you embark on, and peace is taken away from you is not from God. Yes, there might be challenges or tribulations, but they are there for a season, for a time, for a purpose and God who is the author of your life is aware, He doesn't engineer failures or flops. He is the greatest master strategist, so be rest assured He is there with you.

For no temptation (no trial regarded as enticing to sin), [no matter how it comes or where it leads] has overtaken you and laid hold on you that is not common to man [that is, no temptation or trial has come to you that is beyond human resistance and that is not [a]adjusted and [b]adapted and belonging to human experience, and such as man can bear]. But God is faithful [to His Word and to His compassionate nature], and He [can be trusted] not to let you be tempted and tried and assayed beyond your ability and strength of resistance and power to endure, but with the temptation, He will [always] also provide the way out (the means of escape to [c]a landing place), that you may be capable and strong and powerful to bear up under it patiently. -1 Corinthians 10:13. AMPC

Abraham was a man of Purpose, he believed in God, he had a personal relationship with God, and he understood that whatever God says concerning him is final. For twenty-five years he held onto God's promise for a Son and while he waited, he was at peace.

No unbelief or distrust made him waver (doubtingly question) concerning the promise of God, but he grew strong and was empowered by faith as he gave praise and glory to God.......
Romans 4:20 AMPC

A purpose that has God as its source has peace as its companion. You will suddenly begin to feel this wave of calmness all around you, God always speaks peace to His people. A purpose is given in response to a heart desire and desire leads to inquiry and inquiry leads to acquiring and acquiring leads to fulfillment. Everyone seeks for his own purpose; no one can seek for life purpose for another person. It is an individual affair, not a collective effort. A man who desires a life purpose must desire wisdom and separate himself from every form of distraction and seek God.

The purpose you will not pursue; you will not fulfill. The source of every purpose is usually made apparent for all to see at the end of it all, it speaks louder than words, if it is of God, its good fruits will be made manifests for all to see and come to the knowledge of Him and if it a bad fruit it will also show to all eyes.

Chapter Four

HIS STRENGTH NOT YOURS

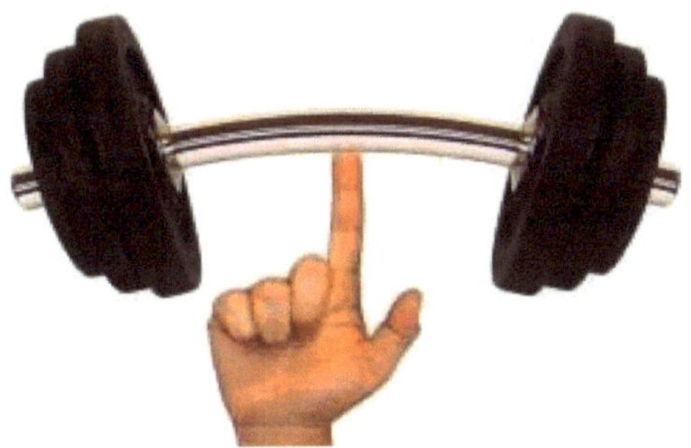

It is important for you not to mistake natural qualities for divine placement. Gods' placement in life is by grace and not by expertise or strength, when God wanted someone to lead His people out of Egypt, He choose a stammered in the person of Moses when He needed a man to build the walls of Jerusalem, He chose a slave boy named "Nehemiah".

Your natural capabilities cannot qualify you for a divine task, divine purpose or assignment require divine strength, and divine strength can only be made perfect in weakness. God will always call you in your weakness so that you can rely on His strength for His assignment. God calls you in your weakness so that you can get to know Him and rely solely on Him, when you do, you will lay hold on divine strength, when you have this divine strength, you will do exploits in your divine purpose or assignment here on earth.

But He said to me, my grace (My favor and loving-kindness and mercy) is enough for you [sufficient against any danger and enables you to bear the trouble manfully]; for My strength and power are made perfect (fulfilled and completed) and [a]show themselves most effective in [your] weakness. Therefore, I will even more gladly glory in my weaknesses and infirmities, that the strength and power of Christ (the Messiah) may rest (yes, may [b]pitch a tent over and dwell) upon me. 2 Corinthians 12:9 AMPC

I have a question for you.

- What motivates you?
- What makes you wake up each morning?
- What drives you and why do you go through life each day?

If you are just like the very few people who have no idea what motivates them in life: you have no idea why you wake up each morning and you have no clue what you want to do with your life. The reason some people wake up each morning is because they have to go to work and the reason they get to work is that they want to get paid and in turn, they get to pay their bills.

In other words, **they are working for money**. Therefore when they are given a choice; they choose to run away from their work. They will choose to sleep longer and sleep later when they do not have to report to the office.

"Motivation is like a fire from within. If someone else tries to light that fire under you, chances are it will burn very briefly." Your motivation should come from within, not from outside. It is not the physical things or money that will motivate you; it is the feeling of ownership, the sense of accomplishment that drives you. Things that should drive you to life's purpose should include the spirit of Excellence, fulfillment, balance, and so on.

The dictionary definition for excellence is "the quality of being outstanding or extremely good". From a Biblical perspective, being outstanding seem most applicable when it is seen as the pursuit of, or abounding in, Christ-like virtue, i.e. "behavior showing high moral standards". I am reminded of Jesus' words, "And when he was gone forth into the way, there came one running, and kneeled to him, and asked him, Good Master, what shall I do that I may inherit eternal life? And Jesus said unto him, Why callest thou me good? There is none good but one, that is, God" (Mark 10:17-18). So, if excellence is the quality of being extremely good and God is the only One that is good, I believe the Bible suggests true excellence is characteristic of people who understand that they have been made in God's image, that they have been "saved" by what Jesus Christ has done on the cross, and they are striving to live in a life-giving relationship with their Heavenly Father, empowered by the Holy Spirit.

Excellence is a spirit and for everyone who is in Christ, excellence is given. It comes with the redemption package. The Bible declares that Jesus obtained a more excellent ministry which is steered by an even more excellent Spirit. The Bible went further to say, "...He is, so are we in this world," 1John 4:17. This implies that we share in the same ministry of excellence with Christ! Glory! Alleluia! We have an excellent spirit.

A great preacher once said, "You do not know your worth that's why you cannot carry your weight!"

When we realize that the same Spirit that distinguished Daniel has been given to us under a better covenant and arrangement, then our outlook on life takes an upturn. Excellence is a spiritual treasure locked away in the chest of our human spirit and we need to go on an adventure to unlock it.

God is always willing to reveal His plans for your life. He didn't make those plans for Himself, He made them for you and me. He has taken it upon himself to lead you to a place of rest, your destiny, your fulfillment, and he can only do that by revealing it to you. It was specially designed for you with your name on it, so go for it, do not allow the cares of this world to deprive you of this calling, this life, this crown, He is waiting for you, He is waiting for that moment when you will come to Him in surrender to ask for His plans for your life. What else do you need? Go for it NOW! He is waiting.

Call to Me and I will answer you and show you great and mighty things, fenced in and hidden, which you do not know (do not distinguish and recognize, have knowledge of and understand). – Jeremiah 33:3. AMPC

Call upon Him now, ask Him, and receive insight so that your joy may be full.

On the other hand, Spiritual fulfillment means the realization of your true self of who you are. Spiritual fulfillment is knowing that you overcome all things that could ever challenge you. It's an understanding that you are complete. It's not something that we can fully speak to in this world. We can't show it to you, hold it up to you and say, "Here is your spiritual fulfillment." It's something you already know inside of yourself, or you know enough about it that you want it.

That realization is an inner experience in which you know that you are not only just enough, but you are always more than enough. That means there's nothing that exists or is in your life that can ever stop you from your spiritual fulfillment.

For me, fulfillment is being right with God.....content, and satisfied.

Chapter Five

LIFE PURPOSE VS LIVING PURPOSEFULLY

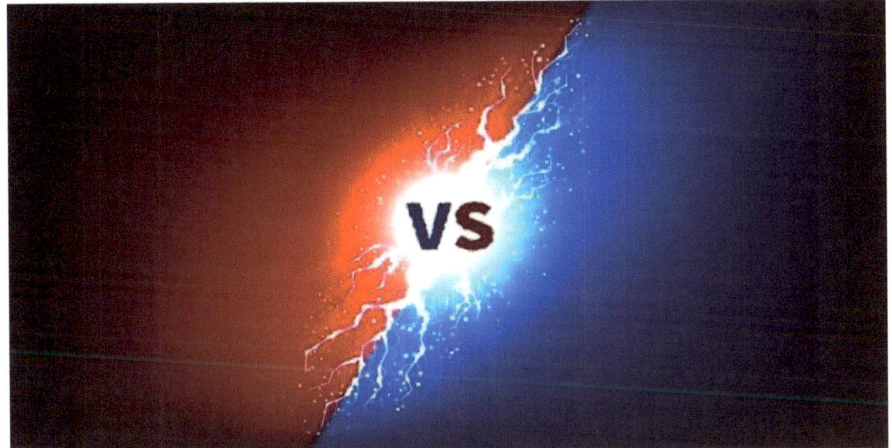

"It is never too late to be what you might have been." George Eliot.

Many people feel intimidated by or resistant to the concept of life calling or purpose. Maybe you do too! Do you worry that having a life purpose means surrendering to a higher power and giving up control of how you spend your time? Do you worry that your life purpose will end up being something unpleasant or taxing? What if your life purpose turns out to be draining or boring? What if it demands more than you are willing or able to give in time, energy, and commitment?

These types of fears are completely groundless. If you could poll everyone on the planet who believes they are living their true-life purpose, I bet they would all say the same thing: "I'm so HAPPY!" Everyone who dares to live their life purpose describes it along the lines of "coming home" or "doing what I was born to do." They do what matters most to them, they enjoy it fully, and it fits perfectly with the rest of their lives. That's not to say that a few sacrifices won't be necessary at times, but I think you'll find that they are not overly painful or difficult. In fact, they may be downright freeing once you let go of your fear and doubt. Don't worry yourself thinking that living your purpose means giving up control of your life. You are always in control of your own life through God. In fact, I want to encourage you to adopt a new outlook for your life – that of "living with God's purpose" rather than "having a purpose".

Living purposefully means DISCOVERING your purpose in Him. God is the author of our lives and destiny, He knows what best suits each one of us, and those plans are of good and to bring us to an expected end. A purposeful life is when you are moving towards a big goal in your life that aligns with your values, passions and makes you happy.

For I know the thoughts and plans that I have for you, says the Lord, thoughts, and plans for welfare and peace and not for evil, to give you hope in your outcome. -Jeremiah 29:11 AMPC

Discovering and living in God's purpose for your life here on earth is very rewarding. You may be surprised to discover just how rewarding a purposeful life can be! Here are just a few of the benefits:

Thus says the Lord, your Redeemer, the Holy One of Israel: I am the Lord your God, who teaches you to profit, who leads you in the way that you should go. – Isaiah 48:17. AMPC

- Greater focus on your daily activities – rather than feeling adrift.
- Increased discipline when it comes to productivity and achievement.
- Passion and motivation! When was the last time you felt excited about your day?
- Personal empowerment – being in control of your own life.
- Meaning and fulfillment. Knowing that your life (and everything you do) matters.
- Energy and vitality! Purposeful living energizes your mind, body, and spirit.
- Peace and contentment. Knowing you are exactly where you need to be.

I could go on and on, but these are probably the most notable benefits of living purposefully. If you've never felt strengthened, empowered, or fulfilled by your activities before, you have not discovered your purpose yet (or choose one that resonates with you). Once you do, every moment of your life takes on greater meaning and passion – rather than seeming pointless and boring. When you walk in God's pre-destined plan and purpose for your life, you cannot fail.

Action is the proof of faith. If you believe in the purpose shown to you by God, act it out! Set out to prove that you believe in it and in his words too. No matter how great a farmer's dream for prize-winning harvest, if he would not take a farmland, secure implements to clear the land, plough, ridge, and sow his seeds, his dreams will have no proof at the end of the day. His fantastic vision or purpose in life will follow him to the grave if he does nothing about it. Vision and Purpose without pursuit are mere wishes. Someone once said "If wishes were horses, even beggars will ride. Actors are winners and winners are Kings. Yes, great is the purpose but great must your drives be, or your purpose and vision will become mere wishes.

Those who do nothing towards their life purpose, groan at the end. The Bible says

The sluggard does not plow when winter sets in; therefore, he begs in harvest and has nothing." – Proverbs 20:4 AMPC

For every vision or life purpose, there is God's provision for it. Therefore, He got you covered because He is your creator and He had a plan for you even before you knew yourself. Thus, all you need or will ever require accomplishing that purpose is made available, there is a provision for it by God. All you must do is run!! Run!! Move! Move! Take those giant steps and make it happen and your crown of fulfillment is waiting for you.

His grace for that mission is available. You can say like Apostle Paul, "I am what I am by the grace of God". What makes a man is the grace of God at work in him, God is your qualification, and without Him you can do nothing. Life purposes are won by the grace of God, He is the one who gets the job done through you, remember, you are His workmanship, He is your creator, created for His purpose- to do His will.

Faithful is He Who is calling you [to Himself] and utterly trustworthy, and He will also do it [fulfill His call by hallowing and keeping you]." – 1Thessalonians 5:24

All your strength is equal to nothing without God. If you must succeed, you must go along with Him. For you to be able to forge ahead, you must be watchful not to stray away from His purpose in your life, keep your eyes fixed on the Purpose.

"And say to Archippus, see that you discharge carefully [the duties of] the ministry and fulfill the stewardship which you have received in the Lord– Colossians 4:17. AMPC

ABOUT THE AUTHOR

Hey, I am Chinedum Erica Mbachu, thefounder of Todays Secret International. I am an Estate Surveyor and Valuer, a Masters' degree graduate in Business Administration, and an entrepreneur.

I am focused on helping women become the best they can be and also build their self-confidence. Likewise, to empower them to build their own businesses and learn how to become financially independent. Whenever I am not engulfed with work, I spend time with my family and friends as I value my relationship with people and help them discover their God-given talents and skills. I also love watching movies and playing Volleyball.

THOSE WHO LOVE GOD
ALL THINGS WORK
TOGETHER FOR GOOD,
FOR THOSE WHO
ARE CALLED ACCORDING
TO HIS PURPOSE.
Romans 8:28